I0391553

Going for Gold

www.ingramcontent.com/pod-product-compliance
Lightning Source LLC
Chambersburg PA
CBHW070434220526
45466CB00004B/1677
9781696192781